Beauty and the Beast

Retold by Annette Smith
Illustrated by Loma Tilders

NELSON PRICE MILBURN

Once upon a time,
there was a rich merchant
who had three daughters.
His youngest daughter
was very beautiful
and very kind.
He called her Beauty.

The two older sisters
were jealous of Beauty.
One day, the merchant
told his daughters some bad news.

"All of my ships have been lost at sea.
Now we have no money.
We must move to a small cottage
in the country."

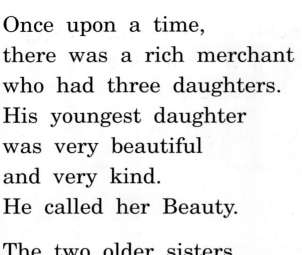

The two older daughters were very angry.
They wanted fine clothes and jewels
and a big house to live in.

But Beauty did not complain.

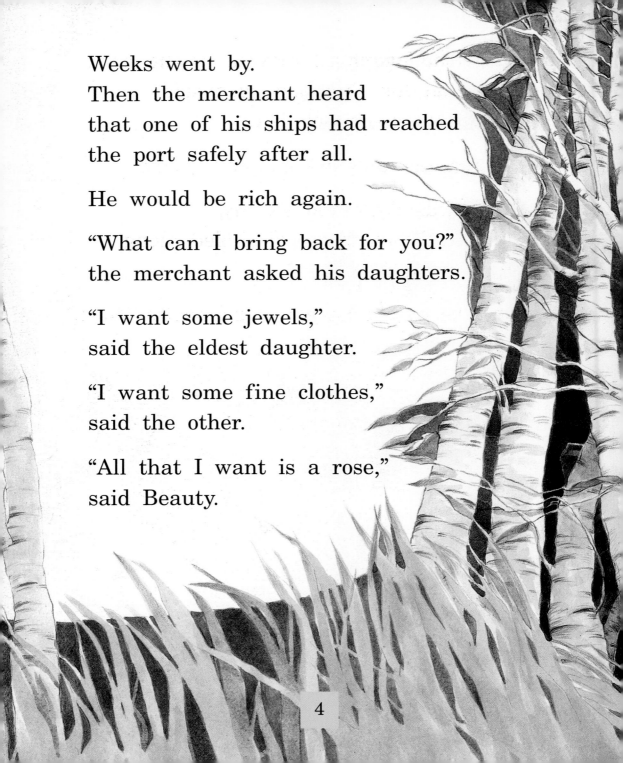

Weeks went by.
Then the merchant heard
that one of his ships had reached
the port safely after all.

He would be rich again.

"What can I bring back for you?"
the merchant asked his daughters.

"I want some jewels,"
said the eldest daughter.

"I want some fine clothes,"
said the other.

"All that I want is a rose,"
said Beauty.

But when the merchant arrived at the port,
he found that his ship had been sold
and there was no money left.

Sadly, he began to make his way home.

The night was dark and stormy,
and the merchant's horse stumbled along
in the icy wind.

He knew he would have to find shelter soon.

At last, he saw a light
shining through the trees.

It came from a magnificent castle.

The stable door was open
for his horse,
and every room in the castle
was warm and bright.

The merchant called out,
but no one came.
It was very strange.

The merchant ate hungrily
from the food on the table.
Then he lay down and slept.

In the morning,
he found that his clothes
were clean and dry once more.

"I wish I could thank
the owner of the castle
for his kindness,"
he said to himself.

As he rode his horse
out of the castle grounds,
the merchant picked a rose from a bush.

Suddenly, there was a loud roar,
and the most ugly beast
the merchant had ever seen
appeared before him.

The merchant was terrified.

"So this is how you repay me
for saving your life," snarled the Beast.

"The rose is for my youngest daughter,"
pleaded the merchant.

"Bring one of your daughters here
to live with me," snarled the Beast,
"or you shall die within three months."

When he arrived home,
the merchant wept
as he told his daughters
all that had happened.

"Do not worry, Father," said Beauty.
"I will go and live with the Beast."

Her two older sisters were glad to hear
Beauty's words.
"It is all your fault," they said.
"It was you who asked for a rose."

The merchant was very troubled
as he rode with Beauty to the castle.

As they drew near,
the Beast appeared with a dreadful roar.

The sight of the ugly Beast
horrified Beauty,
but she said goodbye to her father
as bravely as she could.

Beauty was tired after the long ride.
She was glad to lie down and sleep.
And while she slept, she dreamed
that her goodness would be rewarded.

The next morning,
Beauty was surprised to find a room
with her name on the door.
Inside she found many books
and musical instruments.

"The Beast is very kind.
He can't mean to harm me," she said.

That evening, as she ate her meal,
there was a loud roaring sound
and the Beast appeared.
"Do you think that I am ugly?"
he asked.

"Yes, I do," replied Beauty, trembling.
"I cannot tell a lie.
But you **are** very kind to me."

"I will leave you to have your meal," said the Beast.
"But I must ask you one more thing. Will you marry me, Beauty?"

"I could **never** marry you," said Beauty.

13

Every evening,
the Beast came to watch
Beauty eat her meal,
and he always asked her
the same question.

"Beauty, will you marry me?"

Beauty was no longer afraid of him,
and she enjoyed listening to him talk.
But she could not say 'yes'
to his question.

One day, news came
that Beauty's father was ill.

"Please, Beast," she begged,
"let me go back to my home
to see my father."

"If you do not return,
I shall die," said the Beast.

"I promise," said Beauty.
"I will return in one week."

"Wear this ring," said the Beast.
"When you are ready to come back,
take it off, and you will find yourself
at the castle."

When Beauty reached home,
her father was overjoyed
to see her, but her sisters
were very jealous
of her fine clothes.

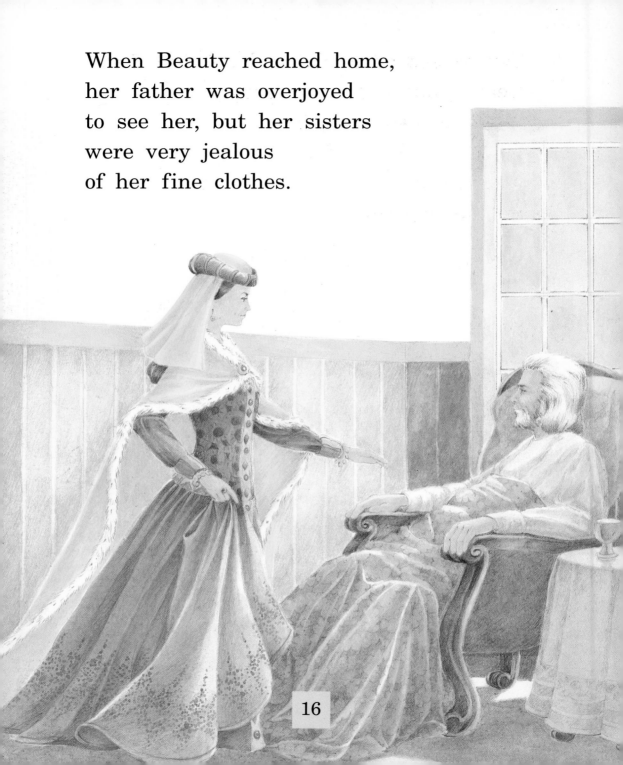

Two weeks after she had left the Beast,
Beauty had a terrible dream.
She dreamed that the Beast
had killed himself
because she had not returned
as she had promised.

Beauty pulled off her ring.

17

In an instant, she was back at the castle.
But where was the Beast?

Beauty searched every room
before she saw him
lying ill in the garden.

"Dear, dear Beast," she cried.
"Don't die. I love you.
I want to marry you."

All at once, the castle was filled
with bright lights
and a handsome Prince
stood beside her.

"Where is the Beast?" cried Beauty.

"I am the Beast!" said the Prince.
"Beauty, you have saved me.
A cruel spell kept me in the shape
of a Beast until you promised
to be my wife."

The Prince and Beauty were married,
and lived happily ever after.

A play

Beauty and the Beast

People in the play

	Reader		Second Daughter
	Merchant		Beauty
	Eldest Daughter		Beast

Reader

Once upon a time,
there was a rich merchant
who had three daughters.
He called his youngest daughter Beauty.
She was very beautiful and very kind.
The two older sisters were jealous of her.
One day, the merchant told
his daughters some bad news.

Merchant

All of my ships have been lost at sea.
Now we have no money.
We must move to a small cottage
in the country.

Eldest Daughter

But I want fine clothes and jewels.

Second Daughter

I want to live in this big house.

Beauty

I do not mind, Father. Do not worry.

Reader

Weeks went by.
Then the merchant heard that
one of his ships had reached the port.
He would be rich again.

Merchant

What can I bring back for you?

Eldest Daughter

I want some jewels.

Second Daughter

I want some fine clothes.

Beauty

All that I want is a rose.

Reader

But when the merchant got to the port,
he found that his ship had been sold.

Reader

The merchant would never be rich again.
Sadly, he made his way back home.
The night was dark, and his horse
stumbled along in the icy wind.

Merchant

I have to find shelter soon,
or I will die of the cold.

Reader

At last, the merchant saw a light
shining through the trees.
It was coming from a magnificent castle.

Merchant (entering the castle)

This castle is very strange.
The stable door was open for my horse,
and these rooms are warm and bright.
But there is no one here.
I am so hungry I must eat this food.

Reader

When the merchant had eaten,
he lay down and slept. In the morning,
he found that his clothes were clean
and dry once more.

Merchant (leaving the castle grounds)

I wish I could thank the owner
of this castle for his kindness.
I will just take one of these roses.

Reader

As the merchant picked the rose,
there was a loud roar,
and the most ugly beast the merchant
had ever seen appeared before him.

Beast (snarling)

So this is how you repay me
for saving your life.

Merchant (pleading)

The rose is for my youngest daughter.
Please, please do not kill me.

Beast

Bring one of your daughters here
to live with me, or you shall die
within three months.

Reader

When the merchant arrived home,
he wept as he told his daughters
all that had happened.

Beauty

Do not worry, Father.
I will go and live with the Beast.

Eldest Daughter

Yes. You should go, Beauty.
It is all your fault.

Second Daughter

It was you who asked for a rose.

Reader

The merchant was very troubled
as he rode with Beauty to the castle.
As they drew near, the Beast
appeared with a dreadful roar.

Beauty

Father, the beast is so ugly
and so frightening.
But do not worry. I will be brave.

Beast (to the merchant)

Go now.
Leave your daughter here with me.

Reader

Beauty was tired after the long ride.
She lay down to sleep.
While she slept, she dreamed
that her goodness would be rewarded.

Reader

The next morning, Beauty discovered a room
with her name on the door.
Inside she saw many beautiful things.

Beauty

The Beast is very kind.
He has given me all of these things.
He can't mean to harm me.

Reader

That evening, as she ate her meal,
there was a loud roaring sound
and the Beast appeared.

Beast

Beauty, do you think I am ugly?

Beauty (trembling)

Yes I do. I cannot tell a lie.
But you **are** very kind to me.

Beast

I will leave you to have your meal.
But I must ask you one more thing.
Will you marry me, Beauty?

Beauty

I could **never** marry you.

Reader

Every evening, the Beast came
to watch Beauty eat her meal.
He always asked her the same question.

Beast

Beauty, will you marry me?

Beauty

Dear Beast, I enjoy listening
to you talk, but I cannot say 'yes'
to your question.

Reader

One day, news came
that Beauty's father was ill.

Beauty

Please Beast, let me go back home
to see my father.

Beast

If you do not return, I shall die.

Beauty

I promise I will return in one week.

Beast

Wear this ring. When you are ready
to come back, take it off and you will
find yourself at the castle.

Reader

When Beauty reached home,
her father was overjoyed to see her.

Eldest Daughter (jealously)

Look at all her beautiful things.

Second Daughter

She should give some of them to us.

Reader

Beauty gave them all her fine clothes
and jewels. For two weeks,
she cared for her sick father.

Beauty (pulling off her ring)

I must return to the Beast.
Last night, I dreamed that
he had killed himself
because I broke my promise to him.

Reader

In an instant, Beauty was back
at the castle. She searched every room
before she found the Beast
lying ill in the garden.

Beauty

Dear, dear Beast. Please don't die.
I love you. I want to marry you.

Reader

All at once, the castle was filled
with bright lights
and a handsome prince stood beside her.

Beauty

Where is the Beast?

Prince (Beast)

I am the Beast.
Beauty, you have saved me.
A cruel spell kept me in the shape
of the Beast until you promised
to be my wife.

Reader

The Prince and Beauty were married,
and lived happily ever after.